Backyard Bugs

Garden Wigglers

Earthworms in Your Backyard

by Nancy Loewen ～ illustrated by Rick Peterson

Thanks to our advisers for their expertise, research, knowledge, and advice:

Sam James
Natural History Museum and Biodiversity Research Center
University of Kansas

Susan Kesselring, M.A., Literacy Educator
Rosemount–Apple Valley–Eagan (Minnesota) School District

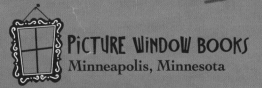

PICTURE WINDOW BOOKS
Minneapolis, Minnesota

Editorial Director: Carol Jones
Managing Editor: Catherine Neitge
Creative Director: Keith Griffin
Editor: Jill Kalz
Story Consultant: Terry Flaherty
Designer: Nathan Gassman
Page Production: Picture Window Books
The illustrations in this book were created with acrylics.

Picture Window Books
1710 Roe Crest Drive
North Mankato, MN 56003
877-845-8392
www.capstonepub.com

Library of Congress Cataloging-in-Publication Data
Loewen, Nancy, 1964–
Garden wigglers : earthworms in your backyard / by Nancy Loewen ; illustrated by
Rick Peterson.
p. cm. — (Backyard bugs)
ISBN-13: 978-1-4048-1144-7 (hardcover)
ISBN-10: 1-4048-1144-3 (hardcover)
ISBN-13: 978-1-4048-1757-9 (paperback)
ISBN-10: 1-4048-1757-3 (paperback)
1. Earthworms—Juvenile literature. I. Peterson, Rick, ill. II. Title.
QL391.A6L55 2005
592'.64—dc22
                                                              2005004060

Printed in the United States of America in Stevens Point, Wisconsin.
072013   0075864R

Table of Contents

A Wormy Morning

It rained hard all night. Now, it's morning. The sun is shining. The grass is green and glistening.

But what's this? Look at all the earthworms on the sidewalks and driveways!

What are they doing there?

Earthworms live in the ground. They make long, narrow tunnels called burrows. When the soil becomes too wet, the worms are in danger of drowning. They leave their burrows and go to the surface.

The movement of the rain confuses them. The worms know they should find a safe place, but they don't know where that is.

Earthworms don't have lungs. They breathe through their skin, which must be kept moist.

Eating Dirt

Let's take a closer look at this earthworm. Its body is made up of many ringed parts, or segments. Can you tell where the head is?

It's hard to tell because the earthworm doesn't have eyes or ears. It does have a tiny mouth, though. If you watch the worm long enough, you'll be able to tell one end from the other.

An earthworm can sense light, heat, moisture, and movement through its skin.

What do earthworms eat? Dirt! Actually, they eat the rotting bits of plants, bugs, and animals that are found in the dirt.

dirt & food

An earthworm's body takes the food out of the dirt it eats. It uses the food to grow and gets rid of the dirt. When the dirt comes out, it's called a casting—in other words, worm poop!

castings

Worms don't have teeth. Like birds, they have gizzards. Bits of sand in the gizzard help grind up food.

Nature's Gardeners

Worm castings might sound gross, but they're actually very important in making healthy soil. Castings provide nutrients that plants need to grow.

And that's not all. The earthworms' burrows let more air and water into the soil. They keep the soil from getting hard.

Earthworms aren't pests. They're nature's gardeners!

One acre (0.4 hectares) of good soil can hold more than one million earthworms.

How Worms Move

Oh, cool! Watch that earthworm move!
First, it stretches long and thin, reaching
as far as it can go. Then, it bunches up,
short and fat. And now it's long again!

An earthworm has two kinds of muscles to help it move. Some muscles go in circles around the worm's body, while others go from tip to tip. The earthworm also has tiny, nearly invisible bristles, called setae, all over its body. These coarse hairs help the worm move, too.

When an earthworm is not moving, the setae are inside the worm's body. When the worm is moving, some of the bristles grab onto the ground while others let go.

15

He? She? Or It?

Earthworms have something that makes them very different from most animals. They have both male and female reproductive organs. But an earthworm can't mate by itself—it still must mate with another earthworm.

Around the middle part of an earthworm is a thick ring called the clitellum. After mating, each worm uses its clitellum to make a shell called a cocoon. The cocoon is made of thick slime and holds the worm's eggs. Within a few weeks, as many as five baby earthworms hatch from each cocoon.

Snails also have both male and female reproductive organs.

17

Besides keeping the soil healthy, earthworms have another important job. They are part of the food chain. Birds, moles, shrews, and other animals eat worms. In many parts of the world, people eat worms, too.

People also use worms as bait for fishing.

A small earthworm can live about two years (if it isn't eaten). Larger earthworms usually live longer.

Wiggling Back Home

It's getting hotter now. The sidewalks and driveways are drying off. If the earthworms get too dry, they won't be able to breathe. They'll die.

How about giving them a helping hand? Put the earthworms back onto the grass so they can crawl back into the soil. They've got very important work to do!

Look Closely at an Earthworm

Look at an earthworm through a magnifying glass.
How many of these different parts can you see?

- Food enters an earthworm through its **mouth**.

- An earthworm's body is made of ringed parts called **segments**.

- An earthworm uses its **clitellum** to form a cocoon.

- Castings come out of the **anus**.

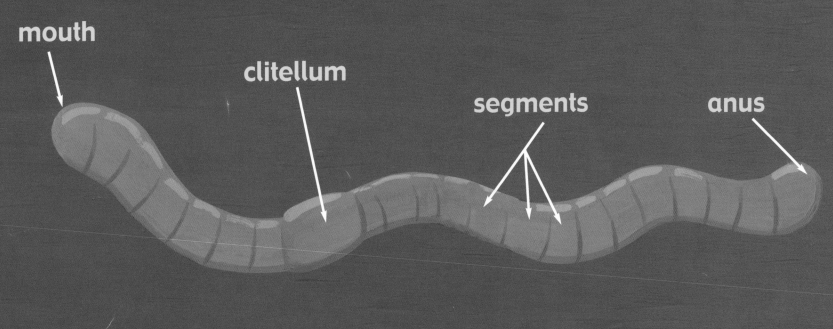

mouth

clitellum

segments

anus

Fun Facts

- More than one million years ago, glaciers destroyed most of the earthworms in North America. Starting in the 1600s, European settlers began to bring new worms to this land. Today, most of the earthworms in North America have relatives in Europe!

- If a bird tries to pull an earthworm out of its burrow, the worm will jab its setae into the soil. The setae hold the worm so well that it may break before coming out.

Make Your Own Worm Farm

Do you want to see how worms live underground? Here's an easy way to do it.

Get two clear plastic containers. One of them should fit into the other one, with about an inch (2.5 centimeters) of space between them. Fill the space between with damp soil. (Don't use potting soil. Get the dirt from outside.)

Now it's time to go worm hunting! Look underneath rocks and logs ... anywhere the soil is moist. If you can't find any worms this way, use a shovel to dig into the dirt.

Put your worms into the dirt between your containers. Stretch a nylon stocking over the top and hold it with a rubber band.

Watch your worms for several days. What do you see? Take careful notes and keep your own scientific journal. When you're done watching, take the worms outside and let them go where you found them. The soil needs them!

Words to Know

castings – Castings is another word for worm poop.

clitellum – The clitellum is the thickest segment on an earthworm's body. It's used to make cocoons.

gizzard – The gizzard is a place in an earthworm's body in which food is ground into small pieces.

mating – When male and female earthworms are mating, they are joining together special parts of their bodies. After they've mated, the worms can lay eggs.

nutrients – Nutrients are things that plants and animals need to stay healthy.

reproductive organs – Reproductive organs are the male and female body parts that are used in making offspring.

segments – Segments are the ringed parts that make up an earthworm's body.

setae – Setae (SEE-tee) are the nearly invisible bristles on an earthworm's body that help it move.

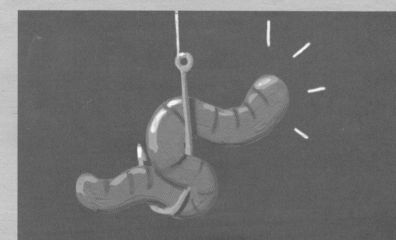

To Learn More

At the Library

Dell'Oro, Suzanne Paul. *Tunneling Earthworms*. Minneapolis: Lerner Publications, 2001.

Himmelman, John. *An Earthworm's Life*. New York: Children's Press, 2000.

Pfeffer, Wendy. *Wiggling Worms at Work*. New York: HarperCollins, 2004.

Schaefer, Lola M. *Earthworms*. Chicago: Heinemann Library, 2002.

On the Web

FactHound offers a safe, fun way to find Web sites related to this book. All of the sites on FactHound have been researched by our staff.

1. Visit *www.facthound.com*
2. Type in this special code: 1404811443
3. Click on the FETCH IT button.

Your trusty FactHound will fetch the best sites for you!

Index

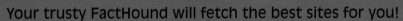

Look for all of the books in the Backyard Bugs series:

Busy Buzzers: Bees in Your Backyard

Bzzz, Bzzz! Mosquitoes in Your Backyard

Chirp, Chirp! Crickets in Your Backyard

Dancing Dragons: Dragonflies in Your Backyard

Flying Colors: Butterflies in Your Backyard

Garden Wigglers: Earthworms in Your Backyard

Hungry Hoppers: Grasshoppers in Your Backyard

Living Lights: Fireflies in Your Backyard

Night Fliers: Moths in Your Backyard

Spotted Beetles: Ladybugs in Your Backyard

Tiny Workers: Ants in Your Backyard

Weaving Wonders: Spiders in Your Backyard